Goal Setting for Success

(Personal Development for Beginners #1)

Eddie de Jong

http://dejong.co.za

Copyright © 2014 - 2015 Eddie de Jong
All rights reserved.
ISBN-13: 978-1495448843
ISBN-10: 1495448843

Contents

Foreword to the second edition 1

Introduction 3
   What is a goal? 3

Chapter 1 – Your Life 9
   Your dreams 9
   Life Areas 13

Chapter 2 - Goal Requirements 19
   Structure of a goal 19
   Write your Goal(s) Down 29

Chapter 3 - Questions 33
   Do you know what you want? 33
   Questions to help you set goals 34
   Questions to help you achieve goals 35

Chapter 4 - Motivation 39
   Pleasure and Pain 39
   Intrinsic and extrinsic motivation 42
   Shit happens 42

Chapter 5 – Take Action 51
   Three Critical steps 52
   Milestones 56
   Resources 59

Chapter 6 – Measure your Progress 61
Celebrate your Successes 62
Learn from your Challenges 63
Chapter 7 – Where to from here? 67
Get to know yourself 67
Summary 69
Are you still worried about what others say? 71
Other books by Eddie de Jong .... **Error! Bookmark not defined.**
Recommended reading .... **Error! Bookmark not defined.**

Foreword to the second edition

This second edition of "Goal Setting for Success" is more than double the length of the original book.

In trying to answer the question "How long should a book be", I tend to strive to make it as long as it should be, i.e. I write everything I feel the reader should know about the subject, but refuse to artificially pad the pages with random thoughts and theory.

Although some of the new topics introduced don't deal specifically with goal setting theory, they cover common obstacles people face when trying to achieve their goals.

The additional information contained in these pages is a direct response to questions asked and problems experienced by my readers. Thank you so much for all the emails sharing your thoughts, comments and suggestions. With your help, I believe this is a better book than what it was before.

I specifically want to thank my daughter Heidi for her input and ideas. It's always great for an author to have someone close with whom he can discuss ideas.

Eddie de Jong

Eddie de Jong

Introduction

"You control your future, your destiny. What you think about comes about. By recording your dreams and goals on paper, you set in motion the process of becoming the person you most want to be. Put your future in good hands - your own."

Mark Victor Hansen

If you really know what it is that you want from life, setting Goals is the way to get there. It does not matter if you want to set career goals, professional goals, business goals or life goals, the goal setting theory in each case remains the same. There is also no difference if you're setting short term goals or long term goals.

What is a goal?

The terms goals and objectives are often used interchangeably. Wikipedia defines a goal as "A *goal* is a desired result that a person or a system envisions, plans and commits to achieve: a personal or organizational desired end-point in some sort of assumed development. Many people endeavor to reach *goals* within a finite time by setting deadlines."

Think about any sport – the participants know exactly what they want to achieve. There's no doubt in their minds. The same applies to a business – they know up front that they want to make a profit and usually set budgets to show exactly how much they want to make and how.

Eddie de Jong

Isn't this setting goals?

Your personal life is no different – the minute you know exactly what you want and set that as the target, objective or goal, you can start focusing on how to get there. Goals in life will help you achieve what you want in a much shorter time than would otherwise have been possible.

When you set a goal, the first thing you must make certain of is that it inspires you.

When you think about your goal and what it means to you, what words to you use and what do you feel? If it's just "okay", it's not good enough. If however you use words such as "Great, awesome, WOW and stunning", and you can't wait to get going on achieving that goal, then the goal is inspiring.

Setting a goal that you're not sure you want to achieve is a waste of time – you will never be motivated enough to achieve that goal.
You might think that people will always set goals based on what they really want.

Unfortunately, that's not true. People often set goals based on what they think they ought to achieve, or, even based on what other people think about them.

Let's use an example of someone studying to become say a doctor. This would be their goal – to become a doctor. If that person has always wanted to become a doctor to help people, it will be a passion and the goal will inspire them. That person is likely to reach their goal and even exceed it.

On the other hand, if the person really wanted to become a musician and his or her parents forced them into studying medicine, the goal remains the same – to become a doctor. Do you think this person will reach their goal?

Goal Setting for Success

A simple reality of life is that many people don't reach their goals. They know what they want, or what they want to do, but somehow the Grand Canyon lies between where they are and where they want to be, and they don't know how to cross it.

In this book, I will show you how to achieve goals and build the bridge to cross over the Grand Canyon to where you want to be. Please pay careful attention to what I just said – I will show you how to build the bridge. You will however have to do all the heavy lifting to get the work done.

Building that bridge can be a daunting task. Don't expect a miracle or any magical shortcuts. If that is what you're hoping for, you'll be sorely disappointed. There will be times that others tell you you're crazy. There will be times where you'll be so scared you can't sleep at night. At times you will even feel that you've failed.

I'm not telling you this to chase you away; I'm simply saying that these things are normal. Every single person that has ever reached their goals has gone through them. Having an experienced guide to show you the way does not remove these feelings and pitfalls; it merely makes it a bit easier.

Make no mistake – reaching your goals and gradually designing and building the life that you want is hard work. There are no short cuts. There is no easy way. This is not some magic formula that will change your life overnight.

BUT …

> If you are willing to pay the price, I will show you how you can make your dreams come true.
>
> Are you ready to take action and change your life forever?

Eddie de Jong

> *"Ever since I was a child I have had this instinctive urge for expansion and growth. To me, the function and duty of a quality human being is the sincere and honest development of one's potential."*

Bruce Lee

Everyone has an instinctive urge for expansion and growth. Personality traits such as being an introvert or extrovert has nothing to do with it, nor is reading personal development books the only way by which a person can develop and grow.

In our society, personal growth starts when we go to school, or even before that, when we learn to walk and talk. Learning new things in your work environment, being coached or even doing the coaching – all these activities lead to a person growing. We all grow in some way or another.

The level of awareness of this growth, and the conscious thought and effort that goes into it, do however often determine the direction and ultimately, the level of achievement or success that is reached.

Any study of successful people will reveal that they don't simply 'go with the flow'. They know (often from an early age) what they want, and then actively go out and get it.

When I tutor school kids, I am often frustrated by their unwillingness to use the opportunities with which they are presented. Here they are in a private school, but they couldn't be bothered to pay attention in class or do homework. I don't think that this attitude is limited to the youth. Many grown-ups simply don't realize that they can determine their own future. They never take responsibility for their lives, but constantly blame others, or make excuses for their 'misfortune', when it is often a direct result of their actions (or in-actions).

This Personal Development for Beginners series of books won't help you believe in yourself, nor can they force you to take action. Those elements can only come from deep within you.

"You can have all the tools in the world but if you don't genuinely believe in yourself, it's useless."

Ken Jeong

Having said that, if you do believe in yourself and are prepared to pay the price, but don't know where to start, this series was written for you.

As you will have noticed, each book is short and (hopefully) to the point. Each book also stands on its own – you can read only one book without having to read the others. I have tried to make them concise, but practical at the same time. An old Chinese proverb says *"A journey of a thousand miles starts with one small step."*

I hope that you will take that first small step with me. If you do, I can assure you that it will be the start of a journey that is spectacular and exhilarating at the same time.

"We would accomplish many more things if we did not think of them as impossible."

Eddie de Jong

Chapter 1 – Your Life

Your dreams

Your dreams …

Where have they gone?

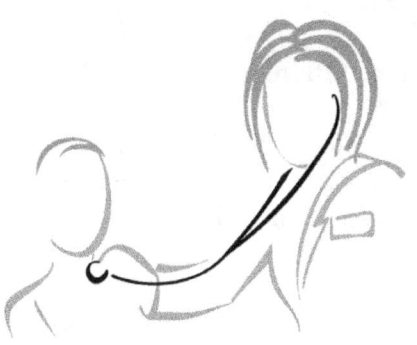

Lost in the wind …

The words above were used in a South African TV advertisement screened by a financial institution.

What did you want to become when you were a child? - A ballerina, boxer or doctor?

We have all had dreams at some stage that somehow don't come true. Can you relate to this? I know I can.

The suggestion of the advertisement was that if you invested with this specific institution, you could make all your dreams come true.

Unfortunately, it's not that simple.

I was watching a movie the other day and the mother said to her son:

"Dreams are just the lies your mind tells you while you're sleeping."

I disagree with this statement. It's this type of thinking that often prevents us from realizing our dreams. How often have you wanted to try something, but never did because others told you it couldn't be done, it's a bad idea or you don't have what it takes? Believe me, this happens all the time.

"One of the lessons that I grew up with was to always stay true to yourself and never let what somebody else says distract you from your goals."

Michelle Obama

Setting goals is most often associated with the work and business environment, especially if it is done in a formal manner. In our personal lives, we tend to use phrases such as dreams and resolutions, especially New Year's resolutions.

I recently came across the following quote:

> *"A goal is a dream with a timeline."*

This is so true. A common problem with dreams and resolutions are that they rarely come true.

There are numerous reasons for this, with the main ones being:

- Dreams and resolutions are not stated in enough detail;

- Once the dream or resolution is stated, it is not looked at again until the next year, or whenever, and then only to realize that it did not come true.

- Others tell us all the reasons why we shouldn't be doing this, and we believe them rather than trusting our own instincts and believing in ourselves.

- To reach most goals you have to change your way of thinking and look at things from a different perspective. Many people have great difficulty in "rewiring" their brain.

- People often have unrealistic expectations about what will happen once they reach a specific goal. You might have a goal of losing weight or becoming debt free. If you think that once you reach those goals it will be easy to keep the weight off or stay out of debt, think again. You will have to continue working at it. When people realize this, they often become discouraged and give up.

I started my career as an instrument technician. Along the way, I discovered computers and was fascinated by them. What started as a hobby became a career, and I soon ran my own software development company – not bad for someone without any formal training in computers or programming!

Eddie de Jong

How did I manage to go from a technician to owning a company that developed strategically important software for large Petrochemical companies? Yes, you guessed it – by setting goals and sticking to them.

The reason I'm telling you this is simply to assure you that the techniques and processes I'm going to describe in the chapters that follow are not some theoretical mumbo jumbo. I have used these methods and seen the results – they work! Fortunately, I am hardheaded and thick skinned enough not to listen to the doomsayers ☺

Amongst many other things, I am a certified Life Coach. The very first session that we do with our clients teaches them how to set effective goals. Time and again I see a transformation taking place. There is no bigger satisfaction than seeing when someone suddenly realizes: "**I can do this!**"

Make no mistake – reaching your goals and gradually designing and building the life that you want is hard work. There are no short cuts. There is no easy way. This is not some magic formula that will change your life overnight.

BUT …

If you are willing to pay the price, I will show you how you can make your dreams come true.

Are you ready to take action and change your life forever?

"When we are motivated by goals that have deep meaning, by dreams that need completion, by pure love that needs expressing, then we truly live."

Greg Anderson

Before we even start with the actual subject of goal setting. There are a number of things you should be aware of. Your thoughts are incredibly powerful shapers of your life. Take some time and monitor what you think of mostly. Do you focus on the negative and dwell on what you don't want?

If this is the case, you might think it's the same as thinking about what you do want. Unfortunately, this is not true.

Successful people focus everything on the goals they desire most intensely. Their conversations and thoughts show clearly where they are going – if you ever speak to a successful person you can't miss this almost obsessive focus they have.

Learn from the masters and start doing the same.

Life Areas

"I believe that being successful means having a balance of success stories across the many areas of your life. You can't truly be considered successful in your business life if your home life is in shambles."

Zig Ziglar

Personal development and setting goals is about change. Before deciding what it is that we want to change on out life, it is often beneficial to stand back and look at our life as it is currently.

To do this, a Life Wheel as depicted below is often used.

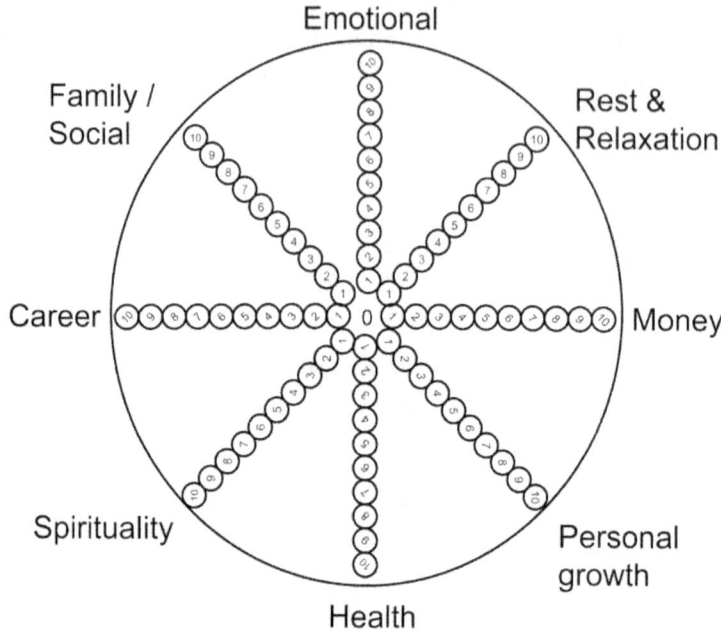

The life wheel has 8 spokes, each representing a key area of life.

Instead of using the wheel with the life areas, you might find it more useful to rather look at the different roles that you have in your life, and rate those. A model for this is shown below.

Goal Setting for Success

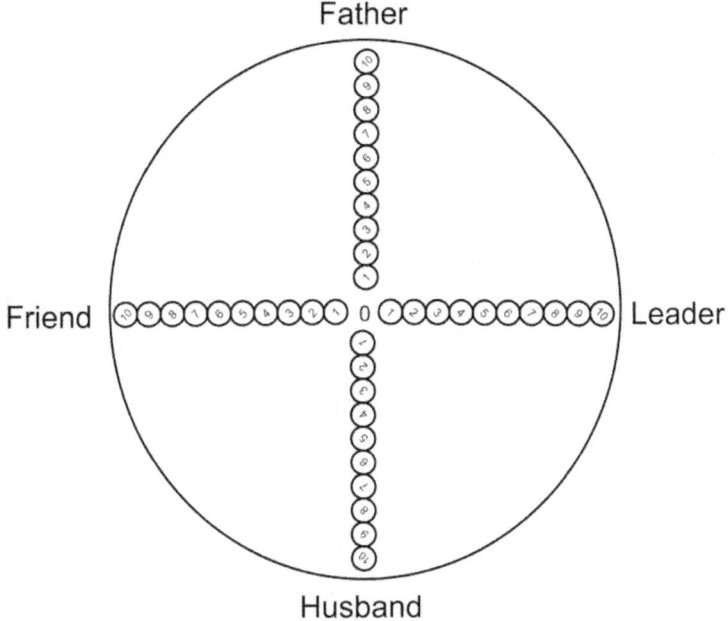

It is important to realize that there are no right or wrong answers here. Use whichever model is more suitable for you, and even change the model if you want to. There are many models that are commonly used.

Take the time now and rate each area of your life on a scale of 0 to 10, with 0 representing non-existent, and 10 being perfection. If you are for example not happy with your career at all, you would typically rate it somewhere below a 5.

If you rate the health aspect of your life a 1, I would expect you to nearly be at death's door, while a 10 might indicate that you are at the top of your game and completely satisfied with your health. It is important that you rate each area based on how **you** feel about that area, and not how you think others would view you.

Depending on your circumstances, it might be tricky to rate some areas. Family / social will typically consist of a number of different relationships. If you have recently gone through a bad breakup with a life partner, how do you rate this area? Try and look at the complete picture and how you feel about it. If the breakup has really shattered you and is affecting all other relationships negatively at this stage, you might score that area a 2 or 3. On the other hand, if your friends and family are really supportive in helping you through these tough times, you might score it a 6 or 7. Don't try and analyze things too much but rather go with your instincts and gut feel.

Once you have rated each of the life areas, join the rating marks on the spokes to give you an overall feel of how balanced your life currently is.

When the scores are joined, chances are that you'll have a jagged shape rather than a smooth wheel. Imagine putting this shape on your car as a wheel and trying to drive with it – it would be a bumpy ride wouldn't it?

The smoother your shape is, the more balanced your life is. If you lead a balanced life, things tend to go relatively easy. On the other hand, if you have one or two areas where you scored yourself a lot less than the others, these areas will hold you back in all the other areas as well.

Once you have a good idea of which areas or roles in your life you are happy with, and which are not going that great, it is time to choose the **one** area or role that you want to change. This is the area for which you are going to set a goal.

You can pick any area of your life to change – it does not have to be the one that you scored the lowest.

This might sound strange – surely it's logical to work on those areas that you scored lowest first? While this is true, it's also possible that you are unable to influence those areas where you scored yourself the lowest. It might even be that you want to change that area, but are not sure how to go about it at this stage.

If that's the case, you should not stop doing what you can. Your happiness or contentment in any area in your life will impact on all the others. No single area sits in isolation. Discontent at work will spill over to your private life, no matter how hard you might try to keep them separate. You are after all one integrated unique human being, and was never designed to operate in different compartments.

Once you start changing and improving one area of your life, the others will be affected. As you gain knowledge and confidence, you will eventually reach a point where you are able to change those areas that you are avoiding right now. If you let that one area block you however, you're not likely to make any progress.

Eddie de Jong

Chapter 2 - Goal Requirements

"Success is about enjoying what you have and where you are, while pursuing achievable goals."

Bo Bennett

Structure of a goal

To have the best possible change of achieving the goals you set, they have to be written in a specific way and meet some essential criteria.

Various acronyms have been used to describe goal setting theory over the years, with **SMART** being the first.

The November 1981 issue of *Management Review* contained a paper by George T. Doran describing S.M.A.R.T goals. The original meaning of the letters were:

- *Specific* – target a specific area for improvement.

- *Measurable* – quantify or at least suggest an indicator of progress.

- *Assignable* – specify who will do it. Achievable was also often used here.

- *Realistic* – state what results can realistically be achieved, given available resources.

- *Time-related* – specify when the result(s) can be achieved.

Over the years, different meanings were assigned to the letters, depending on the context in which goals were used. Goal setting was originally only done in business, but in recent years, this technique has gained popularity as a tool to help individuals achieve what they set out to do. The focus has shifted from setting career goals, professional goals and business goals to setting life goals.

In Life Coaching, the acronym S.M.E.R.T.I.E is seen regularly. Once again, the letters mean different things for different schools of Coaching, with one common use being:

- **S**pecific

- **M**easurable

- **E**vidential

- **R**esponsible

- **T**imed

- **I**nspirational

- **E**motional

I have even seen some people go to extremes and use SMART, PURE & CLEAR, with each letter representing specific criteria that needs to be met when setting a goal.

As far as I am concerned, the last example takes things too far. It's tricky enough to set goals as it is, but to then expect it to meet 14 criteria is madness! You will be busy so long with trying to achieve that, there will be no time left to actually reach the goal.

Based on years of experience in leading teams, mentoring and coaching, I propose a simple yet effective alternative:

I-REST-CA

I'll be the first to admit that I-REST-CA is not as sexy sounding as SMART, but I don't do sexy...

I would rather focus on something that I know works, and is actionable.

The grouping is done partly to make the 'word' easier to remember, and partly to split the elements in importance. The acronym stands for:

- *Inspirational*

- *Responsibility*

- *Evidence*

- *Specific*

- *Time-based*

- *Consistent*

- *Action*

Eddie de Jong

Let's look at the various criteria.

Inspirational

For me, the first and most important is inspirational.

> *Setting a goal that you're not sure you want to achieve is a waste of time – you will never be motivated enough to achieve that goal.*

People often set goals based on what they think they ought to achieve, or even based on what other people think about them. This is a waste of time.

When you think about your goal and what it means to you, what words to you use and what do you feel? If it's just "okay", it's not good enough. If however you use words such as "Great, awesome, WOW and stunning", and you can't wait to get going on achieving that goal, then the goal is inspiring.

Imagine in detail that pursuing this goal will be the only thing you'll do for a long time. Will the effort really be worthwhile? Can you see clearly what it is that you'll be achieving once you've reached the goal. If, after answering these questions, you still want to go for the goal, you'll have the stamina to do what it takes.

To get to a goal that inspires you, you need to know what it is that you want to do with your life, and what or who you want to become. What really drives you? What are you passionate about? Only when you know that, can you set goals to support your life dreams and ambitions.

> *"You can look for external sources of motivation and that can catalyze a change, but it won't sustain one. It has to be from an internal desire."*
>
> **Jillian Michaels**

Responsibility, ***E***vidence, ***S***pecific and ***T***ime-based are the four elements that come into play when you actually set your goal and write it down.

Responsibility

Instead of checking if a goal is Realistic or Relevant like the old SMART acronym did, I use Responsibility instead.

Taking responsibility actually goes a lot further than just goal setting. Taking complete and utter responsibility for everything that happens in your life is required if you want to move from childhood to adulthood.

One would think that this is something that happens automatically when we grow older. Sadly, this is not the case. Look around you and listen to what people are saying. How many men and women in their fifties and sixties are still constantly moaning and complaining about unhappy experiences in their past?

They have not taken responsibility and will always blame either other people or circumstances for their problems. People that are trapped in that mode will never be free and that makes reaching any goal downright impossible.

If you think like that, it's time to let go. Accept the things that you can't change and move on. Take responsibility for all your actions, no matter how difficult it is. By doing so, you will take control of your own life and ultimately, your own destiny.

If you want to set goals that will ultimately bring you success, you have to take responsibility for *all* the actions required to manifest that goal.

Let me use an example to illustrate. I you are currently without a job, you might want to set a goal:

> "In 3 months' time, I will have a job as a manager, and will be earning $ 2,000 per month."

If you still don't have a job in 3 months' time, you have plenty of excuses why you didn't achieve your goal:

- The economy is bad.

- Companies are not hiring.

- There are too many people with my skills and not enough jobs.

The list can go on and on …

What would however happen if you change the goal to?

"In the next 3 months, I will take all the actions required to secure a job as soon as possible. This will include:

- Hand my CV to 5 employment agencies per week.

- Fill in at least 10 job applications on internet job sites per week.

- Find at least 5 corporate websites with job sections per week, and apply for those jobs that I qualify for.

- Tell at least 1 new person per day that I am looking for a job."

In this example, only you can prevent yourself from achieving this goal.

Will these actions guarantee a job?

No, it won't, but the chances are good that if you continue taking these actions, you will find something.

The above goal is based on the experience of a young lady that I recently coached. She had been unemployed for more than a year and was pretty discouraged by the time we started life coaching sessions.

Her goal was similar to the one above and, within 3 months of setting it **and working on it constantly**, she had a job.

If you really want to be in charge of your life, a good motto to adapt would be:

If it is to be, it's up to me!

I want to say a bit more about taking responsibility. If we look at the word, it breaks down to response-ability. In other words, it describes your ability to respond to any given situation.

In any situation, you have three options in responding:

- You can justify – this is when you give reasons, both to yourself and others, about why you haven't done something. These reasons are often untruths.

- You can lay blame – teenagers most often use their parent as the scapegoat here.

- Take responsibility – this happens when you take control of your life and understand that everything happens as a result of action that you have either taken, or not taken.

Do you know in which mode you normally work? The next time you are with people, listen to what they're saying. Are they justifying, laying blame or have they taken control?

I bet that if you identify someone that takes control, you have found someone successful, someone that gets things done and has achieved many of his or her goals.

"In the last analysis, the individual person is responsible for living his own life and for 'finding himself.' If he persists in shifting his responsibility to somebody else, he fails to find out the meaning of his own existence."

Thomas Merton

Evidence

You need to have some way to know whether or not you have achieved your goal. The old term used for this was measurable. If you don't, you won't know when to celebrate!

Setting a goal "I want to be rich" is not measurable. What is rich? Do you mean money or a peaceful, stress-free lifestyle? Don't worry too much about this element – it tends to fall into place automatically once you make sure your goals are specific and time-based.

Once you have formulated and written down your goal, do however check and decided how you will know for sure if the goal has been achieved or not.

"Stop using other people's measuring sticks to rate your success. There will always be someone with more clients, more money, a more successful business... and you'll end up feeling frustrated or constantly chasing success.

Instead,
Set your own measure.
Do what feels good.
Be of service.
Reach your own stars and be happy."

Debbie LaChusa

Specific and Time-Based

All previous acronyms used both the Specific and Time-based elements. The same applies to the new one.

Let's illustrate this principle by using some examples:

> "I want to be a millionaire", or, "I want to be financially independent."

This is a goal (or dream?) shared by many, but how many people actually achieve it?

Let's now modify the goal to read:

> "I want to earn $ 50,000 per month in 2 years' time."

By making the goal Specific and Time-based, it immediately gives us something to sink our teeth into, while at the same time becoming real. With this goal, I can now start asking questions such as:

- If I am to achieve this, how much do I need to earn per month in 6 months, 12 months and 18 months' time?

- What do I need to do to achieve these figures – get another or second / third job? Invest my money? Start my own business? Any combination of the above?

If we start asking and answering these questions, the goal becomes real.

The old SMART acronym used Assignable in its original form. This was later often replaced by Achievable.

> *"Think little goals and expect little achievements. Think big goals and win big success."*
>
> **David Joseph Schwartz**

Yes, it's true that setting unrealistic goals, or goals that are not achievable, will lead to disappointment and failure. The problem is that we often don't know what is achievable and therefore limit ourselves. If I am currently earning $ 5,000 per month, setting a goal to earn $ 50,000 in 2 years' time, without knowing exactly how I am going to achieve this sounds foolish.

On the other hand, if I do set this goal and then start working diligently on achieving it, the detail could very well fall in place and I might even exceed my own expectations.

My advice is to go for something that your gut tells you is possible, without necessarily knowing how exactly you will get there. As you work with your goal and explore possibilities, things will become clearer and you can always modify your goal later.

> *If you err on the side of caution, you will never achieve the best that you can.*

Consistent Action

> *"You must take action now that will move you towards your goals. Develop a sense of urgency in your life."*
>
> **H. Jackson Brown, Jr.**

Our new acronym says I-REST-CA. Just in case you were wondering, no, the REST doesn't mean you can now sit back and relax.

To achieve any goal, it's not good enough to formulate it as per the criteria given, and then write it down as discussed in the next chapter. Ultimately, you need to take action to make it happen.

Taking occasional half-hearted action is not good enough either. It has to be **consistent action**. The more you drive yourself and really go for it, the more likely you are to achieve your goals.

Be inspired. Believe in yourself. Do whatever it is that you need to do and you will achieve success.

Write your Goal(s) Down

"People with clear, written goals, accomplish far more in a shorter period of time than people without them could ever imagine."

Brian Tracy

If you don't write your goal down, you're going to forget it. Sure, if you don't write it down, you may think about it for the first couple of days. The minute things get hectic in your life, or some crises happens, the goal will fly right out of your head, never to be seen or heard off again. This is typically what happens with New Year's resolutions.

However, writing your goal down is in itself not good enough. You **have to** put it somewhere where you **will** see it at least once **every day**. Not only must you see it, but you also need to read it properly. Put it up on your fridge, next to the toilet, on the steering wheel of your car or make it the background on your computer. Make multiple copies if you want to.

The best situation would be to incorporate reading your goal into a daily routine or habit that you already have. If for instance you meditate every morning, add reading your goal to that routine.

When I was still working in the corporate world, one of my functions was to design and implement ISO 9000 quality systems. One of the core principles of implementing such a system is that it must become a way of life, a way of doing things for all employees of the company.

Eddie de Jong

Writing the system is not good enough. When companies are audited on this (typically once per year), the auditors scrutinize every element of the system and make sure that what is written in the manual is actually done in every area.

Your goal should do the same – it is not a once off piece of paper that is created and forgotten. You should know where you're going every waking moment of the day.

In addition to making sure your goals become an integral part of your life, you should write them down in a structured manner. This will assist greatly in achieving them **consistently**, not just every now and then.

If your goal is well structured, it will bring a sense of pride and motivation every time you read it and think about it.

A well-structured goal is more likely to be achieved than an unstructured one, so use as much time as you need to write and re-write your goal until you feel good about it.

Here are some tips to writing effective goals:

- Write in the present tense.

- Use 'I am' rather than 'I will'.

- Include a date – at least a month and a year.

An example incorporating the 3 points above would be:

> "It is the 7th April 2024, and I am feeling great. For the past three months, I have been actively exploring all possibilities in finding suitable work. I have …"

Always write in a **positive** way -

- I am happy / confident rather than I am no longer discontent.
- I am doing … rather than I have stopped doing …

Use words such as:

- I am
- I feel
- I have begun
- Lots of
- I love doing

Avoid words such as:

- I have stopped
- Don't want
- Should
- I will not
- No longer …

Think of what you **do want** and how you **do want to feel**, rather than what you **don't want** and how you **don't want to feel.** Another way of putting this would be to say that you should move toward the positive, not away from the negative.

Make sure the goal is written in such a way that you are fully responsible – no dependencies on others or on circumstances.

Make sure you are in the right frame of mind when you write goals. Be totally in tune with what you want to achieve.

Once you have written your goal, step away from it for a while.

Later, go back, take a look at it, read it out loud and see how it makes you feel.

If you are emotionally connected to it, and it truly inspires you, you are on the right track!

Remember though, this is only the beginning. Now you need to take the **consistent action** to make it happen. More about that in a future chapter.

"Success is not the key to happiness. Happiness is the key to success. If you love what you are doing, you will be successful."

Buddha

Chapter 3 - Questions

"You have to find out what's right for you, so it's trial and error. You are going to be all right if you accept realistic goals for yourself."

Teri Garr

Do you know what you want?

In one of his many books, Stephen Covey said, "Be sure that, as you scramble up the ladder of success, it is leaning against the right building."

Sage advice indeed, but, in my view, very difficult to implement and be sure of.

The road travelled in personal develop is as unique and complex as we individuals are. This means that there is no specific route or formula we can follow to make sure we learn things in a specific order. We will only learn something when we are ready for the lesson, and when that will be depends on your own values, beliefs and experiences.

Many people (including myself) work hard to achieve goals they think they want, only to find out later that this is not the ultimate. I read and implemented Covey's books more than 20 years ago, and they had a big influence in shaping my life. In spite of this, I did not immediately find what I was looking for, what my purpose in life was – that came much later.

Ultimately, your goals and achievements should be in harmony with your inner values and beliefs. You can however only determine your true values as you live life, and that means that your ladder will occasionally be leaning against the wrong building.

Don't let this stop you though. If you wait until you are 100% sure before you do anything, you'll never start. Paradoxically, it's through trying, experimenting and making mistakes that we learn.

Don't try and fight the principle. Be aware of it so that when (not if) it happens, you understand that this is normal, pick yourself up as quickly as possible and move forward.

Questions to help you set goals

It's often tricky to find the right words to write a well-structured goal that inspires you, especially if it's the first time you do it.

The questions listed below will help trigger new ideas in your mind while you are writing down your goal:

- If I had nothing to lose, what would I do?

- What would I absolutely love to have?

- What really inspires me?

- If I were to score this life area or role 10 out of 10, what would be happening in my life?

- How would that make me feel?

- What could I get really excited about?

- What's most important to me in this area of my life?

- What would I do if I had no fear?

Goal Setting for Success

- What else would I love to be, do and have?

- What would still motivate me if I had all the money I could wish for?

- So what specifically would be happening in this area if I reach my goal?

Once you have answered the questions, underline the most important things you've uncovered – that will form the core of your goal.

Don't worry if you don't manage to write an inspiring goal in one session. It often takes time for thoughts and ideas to crystallize. Even if you have come up with a great goal, this can still change and be modified as time goes by.

There's no such thing as a goal cast in stone. It should be a living, integral part of your life, and, as such, it might well change based on changing circumstances.

Questions to help you achieve goals

"Our goals can only be reached through a vehicle of a plan, in which we must fervently believe, and upon which we must vigorously act. There is no other route to success."

Pablo Picasso

Once you have set a goal, you need to make sure it is really what you want. At the same time, you need to check that you are pushing your boundaries and going for achieving as much as you possibly can.

Now is the time to stand back and look at your goal critically. If you are not 100% convinced that this is worth your while doing, modify it until it is worthwhile, or even scrap it if you are not absolutely convinced that this is what you want.

I said earlier in the book that the A of SMART (achievable) is not that important to me. What is more important is the emotional investment you make in your goal.

When you stand back and look at your goal, think about how you feel about this goal. How strong is the emotion? Are you merely feeling OK about it, or do you use words such as great, ecstatic, awesome or passionate? The stronger you feel about your goal, the more likely you are to achieve it.

Achieving a goal is going to take time and effort – for everything worthwhile in life, there is a price to pay.

These questions will help you determine if the price you're going to pay is worth it:

- What difference would this make in my life?

- Is this a 'should do', or is it something I'd genuinely like?

- Am I willing to go all out to achieve this goal?

- How will I know that I've reached this goal?

- If I achieved this goal, will it substantially improve my life?

- Is this challenging enough for someone like me?

- What if I doubled that?

- How would this affect other people in my life?

- Do I think this represents a real stretch for me?

- How does the idea of having this goal make me feel?
- What will I be able to do if I achieve this?
- How could I make this goal even more inspiring?
- Am I really pushing myself enough here?
- Once I have achieved this, what would I do then?

Eddie de Jong

Chapter 4 - Motivation

"I think goals should never be easy, they should force you to work, even if they are uncomfortable at the time."

Michael Phelps

Pleasure and Pain

We are all motivated by only two things – pleasure and pain. Normally, it's a combination of the two, but, interestingly enough, pain is often the more powerful motivator of the two.

Let's use our example goal of wanting to become financially independent to illustrate.

People have many reasons for having this goal – they might want a bigger house, fancier car or better schooling opportunities for their kids. All of these are pleasure motivators.

If your current house is in a dodgy neighborhood where you don't feel safe or your car is constantly breaking down making you late for appointments, the pain of dealing with this will motivate you to do whatever is required to get away from the pain.

When you are setting goals, it is important for you to understand what is motivating you. There will be times that you will feel discouraged about achieving your goal. This could simply be as a result of your emotional state due to events or circumstances in your life.

Whatever the reason, there will be times that you have to dig deep to keep on going.

Knowing what motivates you most strongly will help tremendously in those situations.

Sitting back and asking "What will it be like if I don't reach this goal?" and "How will it be if I reach this goal instead?" will reinforce the reasons why you set this goal in the first place, and help you get going again.

A bend in the road is not the end of the road…
Unless you fail to make the turn.

Although being motivated by pain is a powerful reason for changing things, it does bring with it some dangers that you need to be aware of:

- Working towards a goal to avoid pain often evokes fear, anxiety and self-doubt.

- Trying to avoid pain could lead to you merely trying to survive rather than to thrive.

- Once you have alleviated the pain to a certain degree, it might not be strong enough anymore to motivate you to continue toward reaching your ultimate goal. The same is actually true if you are motivated by pleasure. As you change your live and reach at least part of your goal, the motivation might decrease, resulting in you not getting to where you wanted to go in the first place.

Often, setting a specific goal and not reaching it is viewed as failure and discourages people from trying again.

Is it really failure?

I don't see it as such. If you set a goal and start moving towards it, you have already made changes and improved your situation. This is progress and, if anything, proves that you can do what you set your mind to. If at some stage you don't follow through, or don't reach the exact target you've aimed for, that fact remains that you have made progress. Often, circumstances beyond your control or unexpected events will stop or delay your progress. This is actually normal and is to be expected. Has life ever gone exactly the way you envisaged it? Why would reaching your goals be any different?

When that happens, it's time to re-evaluate your goal. As you have had some experience in finding out what it takes to reach the goal and you might even have seen some of the benefits, you are in a better position than before to decide what you want to do.

Here are some options:

- Leave the original goal as is, and modify the timeline.

- Make some modifications to the original goal and / or timeline.

- Decide you've gone far enough in achieving this goal and set a new one – in the same life area or a different one.

The critical aspect here is not to say "I can't do this" and stop working on improving your life.

"Don't be afraid to fail, be afraid not to try."

Unknown

Intrinsic and extrinsic motivation

Intrinsic motivation compels us to work at something because the inner value of the activity is personally fulfilling and meaningful.

Extrinsic motivation is any outside force that drives you to do something. This could be anything from recognition to your paycheck.

Studies have shown that intrinsically people will:

- Put in more effort.

- Try different ways to succeed.

- Be more persistent.

- Learn more deeply.

This is why it's important to use words such as great, awesome and stunning when defining your goals.

Shit happens

"Life's up and downs provide windows of opportunity to determine your values and goals. Think of using all obstacles as stepping stones to build the life you want."

Marsha Sinetar

The number one reason why people don't reach their goals is over commitment. I call it the *"I want it all and I want it now!"* syndrome.

We tend to get so enthusiastic about improving our lives that we try and do too many things at the same time. You might have set goals to exercise more regularly, take on extra studies to qualify for a better job and start meditating daily. Have you done that in the past, or even when you started reading this book?

The reality is that making meaningful lasting change is a slow process and it is best tackled by using baby steps. You can't run before you can walk. They key to personal development success lies in taking small steps **consistently**, and to keep it up, day in and day out.

If you look at the life areas and you feel that there are a number of them where you want to change, my advice is to start by choosing **only one**. Once you have defined your goal and the action steps required have become routine and a habit, then you can think about adding another goal. This is really a situation where the expression 'least is most' holds true.

> *"People are remarkably bad at remembering long lists of goals. I learned this at a professional level when trying to get my high-performance coaching clients to stay on track; the longer their lists of to-dos and goals, the more overwhelmed and off-track they got. Clarity comes with simplicity."*

Brendon Burchard

If you want to learn more about how daily, small steps can dramatically change your life, I highly recommend reading *The Slight Edge* by **Jeff Olson** (http://tinyurl.com/peox6fu). This is one of the best personal development books I have read. I always have a stack of this book in my study, and give it as gifts to all my new coaching clients.

The second reason why people don't reach their goals is because shit happens.

Life is unpredictable. Just as you think you have things in control, and everything is running smoothly, something will upset the apple cart and your goal will fly out the window.

> *"It must be borne in mind that the tragedy of life doesn't lie in not reaching your goal. The tragedy lies in having no goals to reach."*

Benjamin E. Mays

At this stage you may well ask:

"If I follow all the steps outlined so far in great detail, will that guarantee that I'll reach my goal?"

The answer to that question is unfortunately "No".

Before you all start shouting that you want your money back, let me explain.

Nothing in life is predictable.

Murphy's Law sums it up: "If anything can go wrong, it will"

As you set your goal and start your journey by doing all the required actions consistently, something **will** happen and, in the wink of an eye, everything will change.

Expect it. Count on it. There's no getting away from it. This is one of life's laws that we simply can't get away from, no matter how hard we try.

Also accept that this is normal, and that it's not the end of the world.

Goal Setting for Success

Let me repeat: Things will go wrong, and there will be times that you don't manage to stay on track with your goals, no matter what you do or how hard you try.

This is normal, and it happens to everyone.

Unfortunately, unexpected events is another reason why people don't achieve their goals, even if they have followed everything that we have been talking about.

Unexpected events or circumstances are typically those that prevent you from doing the actions steps that you had planned.

When this happens, many people will be discouraged and start doubting themselves. It might not necessarily be an unexpected event that throws people off track. Maybe the timelines you set with your goal were not realistic to start off with, or things are more difficult or take longer than what you thought.

Irrespective of the reason, giving up on your goal at this stage is only one of several possible choices you have in this situation.

When you get derailed from your plan, and it will happen, don't get discouraged and convince yourself that you can't do this. You **can** do this!

Instead of giving up, follow these simple steps instead:

> Determine the cause of the problem – this could either be external factors over which you had no control, or internal ones where you simply misjudged the time or difficulty of tasks.
>
> 1. If the factors are external, check if the timelines on your goal and / or milestones have been impacted and adjust these if necessary. So what if you're going to reach your goal a bit later than what you originally thought. Is it really that big a deal? Once you have adjusted the timelines, simply pick up where you have left off and carry on doing what you need to do to reach your goal.

2. If the factors are internal, you'll probably have to spend some more time to determine the cause. Here are some possibilities you might want to consider:

   a. Timelines set overly optimistic. You expected to be able to do things a lot quicker.

   b. Your goal might not be as inspirational as you initially thought

   c. Your priorities might even have changed and this goal is no longer as important to you as when you set it.

   d. Your goal might not be specific enough

   e. Your milestones may not be specific enough

Once you have identified why you're not managing to reach your milestones and are therefore not going to reach your goal, change whatever it is that you need to change. It could be timelines, the wording of the goal or setting different milestones.

At this stage it's even possible that you decide to discard the original goal. If you do that, don't stop following your dream – simply replace the goal that doesn't work for you anymore with one that does.

Very, very important, so listen up. When you follow the process I've just outlined, the key is **not** to see the situation as a failure.

I repeat – this type of situation is normal, and is **not** a failure. Get your head around this concept – if you understand this, it might well be the main reason why you succeed in achieving all your goals in future.

When things don't go as we had expected, when things are more difficult than we anticipated – these are the times that we as humans grow and become stronger. Personal development does not happen when you're gently cruising in your comfort zone, no worry in the world, taking each day calmly as it comes along.

Yes, it's good to have those days, and we need them to rest, but that's not when we grow.

Real growth takes place in times of adversity. You determine how much you grow by the choices you make in those times.

In fact, at the stage that you realized you're not on track with your goal, you have already grown and learnt new things. The very act of analyzing why things went wrong is in itself a learning process.

Thomas Edison made many attempts at creating the lightbulb. Some people say 1000, some say 2000. The number is not important.

Urban legend says that a reporter asked Edison if that means he had failed 1000 times.

Edison's answer? – "I did not fail. I've learnt how not to make a lightbulb in 1000 different ways."

In conclusion: The question is not whether or not you're going to reach your goals. The question is how many new things you are going to learn along the way.

I want to illustrate this point by 3 examples that I have recently witnessed.

My daughter wanted to lose weight. To achieve this and to make sure it's sustainable, she set up milestones and action plans that incorporated holistic healthy living principals including gym, yoga and eating healthily for a period of a year.

About 3 months into the program, her car broke down, and they suddenly didn't have water at home due to a burst water main in the area. The water problem took 3 days to be fixed, while the car was operational again after 2 weeks.

These problems turned her whole schedule upside-down. She couldn't get to gym and yoga, and cooking at home wasn't possible without water, so she had to resort to bought meals which often included fast foods.

Once everything was back to normal, we simply sat back and decided that the time she had 'lost' with her goal wasn't significant, and she easily went back to the routine she had designed to meet her goal. The end result was that she lost 27 kg; the weight is staying off even though the year is over and, most importantly, she feels good about herself. She has in fact made a major change to her life for the better.

She told me later that when she got back on track after all the shit that happened, she realized that this was what had tripped her up previously. She had tried to lose weight before, but when her routine was disrupted by whatever events, she never managed to get back on track.

The second example involves a coaching client that set a goal for reading the Bible from cover to cover in a year. To do this, he followed a program that involved daily reading. Like my daughter, he had set this goal for himself in the past, but never managed to complete it.

Sure enough, during the course of the year, he had to go to another country for 2 weeks to sort out a problem. As things were hectic and involved long hours, he fell behind with his daily reading. When things returned to normal, he was very despondent and wanted to stop going for his goal. As it was, he had to work very hard at getting his daily reading done, and felt it would be impossible to catch up the two 'lost' weeks.

Goal Setting for Success

After discussing this, he decided to simply skip the two weeks and carry on with his daily reading routine from that day onward. Needless to say, he completed the rest of the year's reading and feels good about achieving what he set out to do.

At the end of the year, he went back and read the chapters that he had missed out on. The key here was that he didn't stop, but carried on taking the daily actions required to reach his goal.

The third and last example is one that I mentioned earlier in this book, and involved a coaching client that came to me at a stage where she had been without a job for more than a year. Understandably, she was down and couldn't see a way out of her dilemma. She had even resorted to consulting with traditional African witchdoctors for spells and potions to help her get a job.

We set up a goal for her defining the actions that she committed to doing every day, all aimed at getting her resume in front of as many potential employers as possible. In short, she took ownership of her own destiny and didn't wait around for something to happen.

Within three months after setting the goal, she had a permanent position.

You can't do anything about the curve-balls life is going to throw your way,

BUT

You can decide how you're going to react to those curve-balls.

For me, the interesting aspect of her achieving her goal is not so much the fact that she got a job, as the way in which her taking responsibility for her own life had transformed her.

Eddie de Jong

During our coaching sessions, she repeatedly told me how people around her commented on how she had changed – she was radiating a confidence and energy that couldn't be missed, yet her circumstances had not changed.

BUT ...

Her attitude and how she chose to react to those circumstances had.

YOU **can** change your life.

Are you willing to take on that responsibility?

"Experience is not what happens to a man; it is what a man does with what happens to him."

Aldous Huxley

Chapter 5 – Take Action

Successful people maintain a positive focus in life no matter what is going on around them. They stay focused on their past successes rather than their past failures, and on the next action steps they need to take to get them closer to the fulfillment of their goals rather than all the other distractions that life presents to them.

Jack Canfield

In a sense, you are already taking action by reading this book. You might even have written down your goal as per the format. Although both these steps is a good start, it's not enough.

Think of any successful person that you know, or at least know of. How did they achieve that success? They had a specific goal, and they worked on it **every** day. Not only do they know goal setting theory, they also know how to achieve goals and objectives. It does not matter whether their goals and objectives are career goals or life goals, short term goals or long term, they take action every day and achieve those goals.

There are many reasons why people don't achieve their life goals – I don't want to discuss these in detail - that would take another book, and I'm sure you'll be bored out of your skull.

Three Critical steps

If I had to summarize goal setting theory in three steps, they would be:

1. *Find a goal that inspires you and write it down.* I you can do it in the full format as I've taught you, that's great, but don't let that hold you back. If you can only write down a very basic goal right now, it's a start, and that's what's important. You can always refine it later.

2. Plan steps, or **at least one** step that you're going to take **today** to reach your goal.

3. Take action on this goal every day.

Even these three steps will be more than what some are able to take right now.

Let's start with the first one – Find a goal that inspires you and write it down. I've specifically said that you can write down a very simple goal right now, so if you don't want to go into the detail explained earlier, that shouldn't stop you. You might want to start with simple short term goals to get the ball rolling.

Put this book to one side and write down your goal now!

Have you still not followed my instruction above?

If not, what are you thinking right now?

- I don't have the time.

- I'll do it tomorrow after I've thought about it a bit more.

- This is silly, I need to be in the right frame of mind.

- I need to do the Life wheel first and then only can I decided which area of my life I want to tackle first.

- I want to do it properly and for that I need to reread the book and apply the principles.

- I need to be sure of my goals in life before I commit to anything.

- I'm still not sure enough about how to set goals, or how to achieve goals.

If you did not take out a piece of paper and write a goal for yourself, you are probably unsure or scared of something – the unknown, failure, not doing it right? You might also simply be resisting change or don't believe in yourself.

All of these reactions are normal. We all have them to some degree or the other. Courage is not the absence of fear, it's acting in spite of fear. If what I've described above applies to you, you've already made progress – you've learnt something about yourself and how your mind works. Knowing this is the first step to overcoming those fears.

If those fears are stopping you right now, please ask yourself "What do I have to lose?"

If you stop reading for a minute and scribble some random goal on a piece of paper right now, what could go wrong? Nobody will hold you to it. No-one will think worse of you. Only you will know and only you will decide if you want to take it further. You are 100% in control.

So, I ask you again:

Put this book to one side and write down your goal now!

When we set goals, it often consists of a number of smaller action steps that have to be done over a period of time. It is essential that we break the goal down into smaller steps or milestones, each with their own timeline.

Do this now for the goal you've written down. I specifically want you to define one *small* step that will be easy to do every day.

If your goal is health, weight or fitness related, do something like "I will drink one glass of water when I get up in the morning" or "I will walk 300 feet every afternoon."

If it's a financial goal you might want to put away 50c every day.

The exact goal or the size of the steps are not important if you struggle to get going with goal setting. To get going with something is.

Setting a miniature goal like we've just done, and then taking that action every day, is a good way to start getting into the habit of setting goals and taking the action every day until you've reached what you aimed for.

Even if you're past the stage that you're too scared to start, the principles still apply. Simply adjust them to a bigger scale.

As you practice these three steps regularly, start building on them. Apply the rest of the content of this book in stages. Once you've reached a certain level and things become more automatic, read or skim through the book again and add new stuff.

Maybe it's an idea to set a monthly reminder on your calendar to do just that?

Goal Setting for Success

It really happened:

One of my coaching clients, a student, had set a goal that he wanted to become self-sufficient after his graduate studies in a year's time. His father wanted him to continue post-graduate and would pay for it, but he wanted something different and be 'free'. His first action step for the goal was to work out an expense budget.

When I asked him at the next session if he had done this, he hesitated and then said "Sort of." Further discussions revealed that he got so scared when he saw the amounts involved, that he stopped the exercise.

I explained to him that completing the budget properly carried no risk whatsoever. In fact, none of the actions he would take in the year to prepare for his freedom carried any risk. There would only be a risk at the end of the year when he had to tell his father, and actually go out on his own. By that time, he would know in detail what this move entailed.

Taking action toward achieving your goal on a daily basis should, in the beginning at least, include reading your goal. I recommend that you do this out loud with a smile on your face and with as much feeling as possible. As with any recommendations in the book, it's not the end of the world if you decide not to follow them to the letter. We are after all unique, and what works for one will come across as ridiculous and false for another.

However you decide to do it, make sure that your goal becomes a part of you. You should think about it often. It should not be a forgotten piece of paper that you 'discover' a year or two from now and throw in the trash.

Dream it and live it – that's the only way to make it come true.

Milestones

In the previous section, I briefly touched on milestones. These are the small action steps you have to take over a period of time to ultimately reach your goal. Once again, this technique can be applied irrespective of whether you are setting professional goals, business goals or your own personal goals in life.

Milestones can be seen as 'mini' goals, each with their own timeline.

Breaking your goal into smaller steps, each with their own timeline will achieve two things:

- It will make the goal less daunting.
- It will allow you to measure your progress and make adjustments

Let's discuss these:

1. It will make the goal less daunting.

If I set myself a goal of writing a 100 page book in three months, it's difficult to really grasp what I need to do to reach that goal.

100 pages might not sound much, but it is roughly equivalent to 15 to 20 thousand words. That's a lot!

When I first decided that I wanted to write a book, and realized how many words I would need to write, I was thinking "Whaaaat? How am I ever going to get this done?"

I was remembering the essays I had to write at school. Back then, 300 or 500 words were a lot. Now I was suddenly faced with 20 thousand words!

If I however decide that I'm going to write 5 days per week which gives me 60 writing days in the three months.

This would mean that I have to write between 250 and 333 words per day.

I can do that!

Once you know the specific detailed actions you have to take, schedule your time and do the work!

Before we move onto the next topic, I want to ask a question: "Why do people generally have blue Mondays?"

Yes, if you hate your job you're not going to want to go back to work on a Monday, especially after a good weekend, but there is another, psychological reason.

A weekend breaks our normal routines and habits. Because of this break, we find it difficult to get back to "normal" on a Monday morning.

You might want to take this into account when you create your milestones. In my example, I said I'll be writing 5 days a week. This means that it's possible that I'll struggle to get back into writing on a Monday.

If you find this to be the case, you might want to consider setting your schedule to take action on your goal every day including weekends.

I'm not saying that you should never relax. To work at my goal every day and still have a good weekend, I could decide to write 100 or even 50 words per day on Saturdays and Sundays. This will not break my writing habit, while at the same time allow me to do other things on the weekend.

The second thing breaking your goal into milestones will do is:

2. It will allow you to measure your progress and make adjustments

If you don't break your goal down into milestones, how will you know if you're on track?

With a goal of 100 pages in 3 months, there's no way that I could know if I'm ahead or behind schedule at any given time. It's likely that I'll only realize that I'm not going to make it close to the end of the 3 months, and by then it's too late. There won't be enough time left for me to catch up.

If I however know that I need to write 250 – 333 words per day, I can easily see at the end of each week whether or not I'm on schedule. If I do fall behind, it should be relatively easy to catch up on Saturday and Sunday, the days that I didn't schedule to write, or scheduled to write less.

Some people like to go into a lot of detail when planning their action steps. Personally, I tend to take a broader approach, but this also depends on the goal and the detail actually required.

I teach various higher grade subjects as a hobby. One of the school's requirements is that all tutors submit a lesson plan for the whole year. Some tutors will go as far as detailing exactly what they will be doing each and every lesson. For me, this is way too much work (I am essentially a lazy bum!☺)

I simply take the number of pages for each subject's text book and divide that by the number of teaching weeks in the year. My lesson plan then consists of a simple table with the week number (or date) and the page number I should have covered by the end of that week. An extra column allows me to write the actual page where I'm at, so I can see at a glance if I'm ahead of or behind schedule.

Neither of the two methods are better than the other. It's simply a matter of balancing your personality and requirements and find a way that works for you.

What is however important is that you know by which date you should ideally achieve your milestone, and also to measure and record when you did in fact achieve it.

If you don't do this, it's likely that you'll find out that you're not going to achieve your goal at a stage where it's far too late to do anything about it. Daily action should include measuring and monitoring progress, and making any adjustments if and when required.

If you do measure and monitor your progress, you will know the minute you're running behind schedule. If you still want to meet your overall goal's target date, you need to do something about it, and fast. Don't let your timetable and milestones slide – doing so will guarantee that you won't achieve your goal on the date that you've set. Make adjustments and do whatever it takes to get back on track.

In spite of your best efforts, there may well times that it's impossible to catch up lost time. In that case, there's nothing wrong with adjusting your goal's due date to a new date that reflects the reality. Doing so is not failing! Don't give up just because it's taking longer than what you thought it would.

Which is better – stopping all action and not moving forward with your goal at all because your original time estimate was wrong, or ultimately reaching your goal, albeit later than what you had hoped for? I hope the answer is obvious!

Resources

In order to reach your goal, you're going to need resources. Typical resources would include things like materials, energy, services, people and knowledge.

Once you've set your goal, it's handy to list all the resources that you're going to need in order to achieve that goal.

Doing so at the start of the process means you can create action steps to obtain those resources that you will need and don't already have.

One way of grouping resources would be:

- People that can assist – These can include mentors, coaches, partners, family and friends supporting you, and specialist in specific knowledge areas.

- Items I already have – physical items could include training materials, exercise or gym equipment, or club and society memberships.

- Internal resources – these are often typical characteristics or attributes that will help you achieve your goal – drive, passion, intelligence, specific knowledge and perseverance are some examples.

- To source – items or knowledge that you'll need but don't yet have. The other categories are a reminder of how prepared you already are to reach your goal, while the items in this one would have to be obtained by setting specific milestones and action steps. Items to source will often have to be done in a specific order.

Chapter 6 – Measure your Progress

"Try to discover the road to success and you'll seek but never find, but blaze your own path and the road to success will trail right behind"

Robert Brault

Throughout this book I have stressed various areas where it's important to write things down – from your actual goal to the detail of your milestones and when you achieved them.

For some, it's enough to write down their goals and milestones, and read them every day. It helps them staying focused and knowing exactly what they need to achieve every day.

For others (like my daughter) however, this is not enough.

My daughter thrives on breaking things down in manageable steps and she LOVES checklists.

This helps make her feel accountable for what she has not done, and often also makes it clear why her goals take longer to achieve than what she had initially planned.

Some time ago, she set a goal to lose 20kg in one year. She broke this down into a list of things she needed to do daily:

- Eat a healthy breakfast

- Eat a healthy lunch

- Eat a healthy dinner
- Eat only healthy snacks
- Exercise
- Limit coffee to one cup per day
- Drink 3l water per day

From this, she created a checklist that she ticked off every day. Once a month, she weighed and measured, recording these figures to make sure she was still on track.

For her, writing the checklist and ticking it daily instilled a sense of achievement, even if there was no other measure available to indicate whether or not she was moving forward – weighing and measuring daily would not help as these indicators can fluctuate in such a short time.

Apart from this, there is enormous benefit to be gained from recording your journey and measuring your progress.

Celebrate your Successes

Remember, life is a journey and not a destination. We are meant to enjoy every moment! Too many people wish their lives away – "I can't wait until…", "I wish it was already…"

The same applies to setting and achieving goals. Enjoy and be proud of the victories along the way and celebrate them. One way of doing this is to set yourself a reward for every milestone reached.

These rewards don't have to be big, but they must be something that's really special to you and that you don't do often.

Noticing and celebrating your achievements will also motivate you to continue when things don't go according to plan.

Life is unpredictable, and will often not go according to plan. The same happens when you set out to achieve a goal. When this happens, don't become despondent and give up. Rather look book at how far you've already come, and know that this is only the beginning of great things.

Learn from your Challenges

Many people know what needs to be done to reach their goals, but get frustrated because, not matter what they try, they can't get themselves to take the action.

A number of the reasons for this have already been discussed, e.g. making sure you have passion for your goal and making yourself responsible for all your actions.

In spite of this, some want the goal with their whole being, but still can't bring themselves to take the action required. If you are struggling with this, it's all the more reason to record your journey and, in this case, your lack of progress.

As you know by now, I don't view this as a failure, and neither should you. Rather see it as a challenge and take the opportunity to learn from it.

The root cause for this type of behavior is often a subconscious resistance to change that is so strong that it overpowers the conscious desire to change. As the resistance is subconscious, it is very difficult to identify and solve.

Eddie de Jong

Behind every intention or desire to change, there is often a 'hidden' intention to do the opposite. For example – if your goal is to become more self-assured, your hidden goal may be to protect yourself by hiding. Unfortunately, our brain is often not our best friend. It will lie to you in order to protect you. The problem with this is that the reason the brain thinks we need protection is often built on its own perceptions. This is not always accurate.

The good news is that there is something you can do to prevent these 'hidden' intentions from holding you back. This is where writing things down comes in.

When you find yourself in this situation, start questioning your thoughts. Ask "Why?" and ask it repeatedly. When you do so, listen to the words you're using. You need to recognize the underlying attachments, desires and fears that are stopping you from reaching your goal.

In doing so, your relationship with the hidden intentions will change from denial to acceptance and in turn, this will take away a lot of the power you brain had on you.

It is important to remember to be kind to yourself throughout this process and to take on a curious, accepting and non-judgmental attitude to your own experience.

Below are some questions you can ask yourself to uncover your hidden intentions:

- What am I afraid will happen if I reach this goal?

- What negative consequences are there when reaching my goal?

- Is there some pain I'm running away from while I'm setting this goal?

- Does reaching this goal 'fit' with the type of person I believe myself to be?

- Has anyone ever told me I can't reach this goal and do I believe them?

- What will I 'lose' when I reach my goal?

- Is there anything that I want MORE than reaching my goal?

- Am I afraid of the change this goal will bring about? Why?

Eddie de Jong

Chapter 7 – Where to from here?

"If you go to work on your goals, your goals will go to work on you. If you go to work on your plan, your plan will go to work on you. Whatever good things we build end up building us."

Jim Rohn

Get to know yourself

Personal Development is a journey of discovery. It is never ending and certainly does not stop by learning how to set goals. Irrespective of all the various skills you learn, the pinnacle of knowledge is to really know yourself. Once you understand why you react and do the things you do, the changes you'll be able to make to your life will be nothing short of phenomenal.

To do this, you need to become consciously aware of your thoughts and actions. Once you achieve this, you can start questioning why you do the things you do, and think the way you do. Then check if your reasons are valid and change your thoughts and behaviors if they're not.

Below are some additional point that you might want to think about or study in greater detail.

- **Find your values and purpose in life.** Your goals will be meaningful and satisfying only if they are truly aligned with your life's purpose and your values.

- **Trust your instincts**. I am primarily a left-brain thinker. If I can't reason something out using logic, I tend not to go for it. In recent years I've learnt to trust my instincts and act on them, even in the absence of logic. Although it was scary at first, the results have been more than worth it. I won't go as far as to say that my instincts are always right, but they are most of the time. When we trust that small inner voice that tells us what we need to do, even if that flies in the face of conscious logic, we are being true to our innermost self and our value system.

- **The past is not a predicator of the future.** We will often not attempt to do something because we've feel we've failed at a similar endeavor in the past. If you do that, you ignore and discount all the learning and experience you've gained over time. In my teens, I was an extreme introvert with zero social skills. Today I am an author and am comfortable with presenting seminars before big groups of people. Need I say more? We all grow and change every day.

- **Always focus on the positive.** Our thought have amazing power over how happy we are. If you constantly focus on the negative aspects of your life, you will be miserable, unhappy, stressed and frustrated. Choose instead to focus on the positive. If you think that you have none or very few positive things going for you, think again. We all have many blessings in our lives – all you need to do is identify them and then focus on them. You'll be amazed at the difference it will make in your life.

Summary

1. Decide for which area of your life you want to set a goal.

2. Brainstorm and design your goal to meet all the requirements of a well-structured goal.

3. Make sure your goal inspires you.

4. Write your goal down.

5. Read your goal every day – use emotion and be inspired!

6. Break your goal down into smaller chunks, or milestones with timelines.

7. Monitor your milestones.

8. Celebrate when you reach your milestones.

9. Take the actions required to get the job done.

10. Don't take on more than what you can comfortably handle.

11. When shit happens (and it will), first get your life back on track. Then sit back, look at your goals and milestones realistically, and adjust if required. Once you have done this, simply carry on with your journey to success, and don't let the detour trick you into abandoning your dreams.

12. Revisit training material regularly, even if you only skim through it. When reading a book or attending any training, we all filter the information through our own experiences and perception. No two people will get the same value from a book or training course. As you learn new things and your perception and understanding of issues change (and this happens every day), you do in fact become a different person. You'll find that if you go

over material a second or third time, you'll suddenly see things differently and pick up new nuggets of information that you can apply to your life.

13. Take consistent action to make your goal happen.

If you battle to find the time to carry out all the actions required to reach your goals and build a better life for yourself, managing your time effectively is a skill that can be learnt.

In the second book in this Personal Development series, *Time Management for a Productive Life* (http://tinyurl.com/pcomkml), I show you how to decide which things to do first, and where it is OK to drop the ball.

We all have 24 hour in a day, yet some people seem to have a fuller, more rewarding life than others, and always get things done. By applying simple techniques, you will have the time to achieve your goals, be successful and be happy with your life.

> *"There are two primary choices in life: to accept conditions as they exist, or accept the responsibility for changing them."*
>
> **Denis Waitley**

Are you still worried about what others say?

As you start working on setting goals in life and changing yourself and your life for the better, you will find people that have something negative to say about your goals or ambitions. I believe that the number one reason for people not becoming the best they can, is because others tell them, in whatever way, that they can't do it.

This is often not because people are inherently nasty, but is caused by ignorance. Many people don't realize that they can, to a certain degree, control their own future and destiny. They simply "go with the flow" and react unthinkingly to their environment and circumstances. People also tend to view life through their own narrow perspective, and simply fail to see the possibilities life itself offers us.

If you are doubted, criticized or even laughed at, remember that you do have a choice as to how you're going to react to this type of attitude.

You can either believe in others more than you do in yourself and slowly sink into the common pool of mediocrity, or you can decide to ignore the naysayers, put your head down and work on becoming the best you can.

If you decide on doing the latter, you will be in good company. History gives us a number of well-known examples of people that were scoffed at by their peers or 'betters', but who, in spite of this, rose above it to become world renown for their achievements.

Eddie de Jong

Being from South Africa, the first example that comes to my mind is ☐ *elson* ☐ *andela*. From being found guilty of treason and sentenced to life imprisonment, to becoming South Africa's first democratically elected President, his journey became a legend and lifted his status to that of an international icon.

Searching for some more examples, I found a list mentioning people such as Thomas Edison, Albert Einstein and Abraham Lincoln. Each of these individuals had been told at some stage in their lives that they we not good enough, yet they went on to achieve greatness.

What made these people different? Put simply, they believed in themselves. They knew they always had a choice, and never gave up dreaming. However, dreaming in itself is not enough. Remember, to achieve your dreams, you have to take action and keep at it ***no matter what happens***.

If the people mentioned on the list could achieve what they did, what is stopping you from achieving to best that you can be?

Twelve Famous People Who Succeeded Against the Odds.
(http://tinyurl.com/ku5qjyd)

1. **Thomas Edison,** the inventor of the light bulb, was told by his teacher that he was too stupid to learn anything.

2. **Louisa May Alcott**, author of Little Women, was turned down by countless publishers who told her no one would ever read her now classic children's book.

3. **Woodrow Wilson**, a Rhodes scholar and president of the United States, didn't learn the alphabet until he was eight; he didn't read until he was eleven.

Goal Setting for Success

4. ***Wilma Rudolph*** contracted polio at age four, crippling her as a child. She was told she would never walk. She decided to become a runner and went on to win three Olympic gold medals and was named the "Fastest Woman in the World."

5. ***Albert Einstein*** did not talk until age four or read until age nine He performed badly in almost all of his high school courses and failed his college entrance exams.

6. ***Abraham Lincoln*** began his service in the Blackhawk War as captain. By the end of the war he had been demoted to private.

7. ***Lucille Ball*** was told when she first started studying acting by an instructor to "Try any other profession. Any other."

8. ***Ludwig van Beethoven*** was initially told by his music teacher that he was hopeless as a composer.

9. ***Cher*** had learning disabilities as a child.

10. ***Michael Jordan*** was cut from his high school basketball team.

11. ***Walt Disney*** was fired by a newspaper editor for lacking great ideas. He went bankrupt several times and was told repeatedly to "get rid of the mouse because there's no potential in it."

Although the heading says twelve people, there were in fact only eleven mentioned on the list, but I'm sure you can add some more names if you feel so inclined.

Thanks for reading!

I write these books because I enjoy doing so, and I love to help people become the best they can be.

If you have enjoyed this book and have found value in it, you might be interested to know that I'm currently giving away this book, _Time Management for a Productive Life_ and _The Power of Habit be Efficient in Everything you do_ to all new subscribers of my blog at http://dejong.co.za

Head over there right now and take advantage of this great offer before I change my mind!

Once you have subscribed, won't you please consider leaving an honest review on Amazon?

Your review can help other potential readers make an informed decision on whether to buy this book or not.

Click here (http://tinyurl.com/pmal88k) to review now.

PS. If you decide not to subscribe or do a review for whatever reason, that's okay.

BUT

Don't you dare not take action on the new things you've learnt by reading this book!

You can change your life and make it what you want it to be,
but only if
you take consistent action.

Other books by Eddie de Jong

Non-fiction

1. Win with Excel
   (http://tinyurl.com/pup6awz)

2. Goal Setting for Success (Personal Development for Beginners # 1)
   (http://tinyurl.com/ltufl4q)

3. Time Management for a Productive Life (Personal Development for Beginners # 2)
   (http://tinyurl.com/pcomkml)

4. The Power of Habit: be Efficient in Everything you do (Personal Development for Beginners #3)
   (http://tinyurl.com/o5ez82b)

5. Personal Development for Beginners: Book 1 - 3: Goal Setting for Success; Time Management for a Productive Life; The Power of Habit: be Efficient in Everything you do
   (http://tinyurl.com/qfmgtqc)

6. Take Action! and Build the Life you want (Action for a better life #1)
   (http://amzn.to/1x3nlPg)

7. Take Action! and Start your own Business (Action for a better life #2)
   (http://amzn.to/1OJ7n5n)

Eddie de Jong

Fiction

1. Velvak's Victory (Bradapol book #1)
   (http://tinyurl.com/q9m7yxh)

2. Velvak and the Bio (Bradapol book #2)
   (http://tinyurl.com/lzjjtx8)

Recommended reading

If you enjoyed this book, you might also enjoy these personal development books:

1. The Slight Edge by **Jeff Olson**
   (http://tinyurl.com/peox6fu)

2. The Goal: A Process of Ongoing Improvement by **Eliyahu M. Goldratt**
   (http://tinyurl.com/pvh5kb5)

3. HOW TO ACHIEVE SUCCESS And Think Like an Entrepreneur by **Mary - Kate Reed**
   (http://tinyurl.com/p2y4y7a)

4. Eat That Frog!: 21 Great Ways to Stop Procrastinating and Get More Done in Less Time by **Brian Tracy**
   (http://tinyurl.com/qjbzr49)

5. The 10X Rule: The Only Difference Between Success and Failure by **Grant Cardone**
   (http://tinyurl.com/q4s98cr)

6. Achieve Anything : Set Goals, Reach Goals and Get Everything You Want (a stress free book to achieve success) by **Mike C. Adams**
   (http://tinyurl.com/ncp6uuk)

7. Unconventional Goal Setting: How To Set Life Changing Goals & Hit Them With 100% Accuracy by **Gavin Weber**
   (http://tinyurl.com/nwvt97f)

8. The Power of Self-Confidence: Become Unstoppable, Irresistible, and Unafraid in Every Area of Your Life by **Brian Tracy**
   (http://tinyurl.com/p6vw9kn)

9. How To Set Goals: Ultimate Goal Setting Guide to Having Your Best Year Ever by **Craig Ballantyne**
   (http://tinyurl.com/qxft336)

10. GMC: Goal, Motivation, and Conflict by **Debra Dixon**
    (http://tinyurl.com/nqw8vk6)

www.ingramcontent.com/pod-product-compliance
Lightning Source LLC
Chambersburg PA
CBHW071754170526
45167CB00003B/1029